A Benjamin Blog and his Inquisitive Dog Investigation

Exploring Rain Forests

Anita Ganeri

Heinemann
LIBRARY
Chicago, Illinois

To contact Capstone Global Library please phone 800-747-4992, or visit our web site, www.capstonepub.com

Edited by Dan Nunn, Rebecca Rissman, and Helen Cox Cannons
Designed by Joanna Hinton-Malivoire
Original illustrations © Capstone Global Library Ltd
Illustrated by Sernur ISIK
Picture research by Mica Brancic
Production by Helen McCreath
Originated by Capstone Global Library Ltd

Library of Congress Cataloging-in-Publication Data
Ganeri, Anita, 1961- author.
  Exploring rain forests : a Benjamin Blog and his inquisitive dog investigation / Anita Ganeri.
    pages cm.—(Exploring habitats, with Benjamin Blog and his inquisitive dog)
  Includes bibliographical references and index.
  ISBN 978-1-4329-8779-4 (hb)—ISBN 978-1-4329-8786-2 (pb) 1. Rain forest ecology—Juvenile literature. 2. Rain forests—Juvenile literature. 3. Rain forest animals—Juvenile literature. I. Title.
QH541.5.R27G36 2014
577.34—dc23   2013017416

Acknowledgments
The author and publisher are grateful to the following for permission to reproduce copyright material: Alamy p. 22 (© John Warburton-Lee Photography); FLPA pp. 9 (Minden Pictures/Kevin Schafer), 15 (Imagebroker/Stefan Huwiler), 20 (Minden Pictures/Chien Lee), 21 (David Hosking), 25 and 29 top (both Silvestre Silva/Holt); Getty Images pp. 10 (Oxford Scientific/Richard Packwood), 24 (Arco Images/Schulz Gerhard; Naturepl.com p. 27 (Anup Shah); Photoshot pp. 11 (© NHPA/Martin Zwick), 19 (© NHPA/Joe McDonald), 23 (© NHPA/Adrian Hepworth); Shutterstock pp. 4 (© Christopher Meder), 5 (© Alexey Stiop), 6 (© Vitaly Titov & Maria Sidelnikova), 8 (© gary yim), 12 (© kkaplin), 13 (© tome213), 14 (© Photogrape), 16 (© Chris Alcock), 17 (© Karen Givens), 18 (© Natali Glado), 26 (© pupunkkop), 29 bottom (© Karen Givens); SuperStock p. 7 (Minden Pictures).

Cover photograph of a tropical rain forest reproduced with permission of Shutterstock (© Eky Studio).

We would like to thank Michael Bright for his invaluable help in the preparation of this book.

Some words are shown in bold, **like this**. You can find out what they mean by looking in the glossary.

Contents

Welcome to the Rain Forest!

Hello! My name's Benjamin Blog and this is Barko Polo, my **inquisitive** dog. (He's named after the ancient ace explorer **Marco Polo**.) We have just returned from our latest adventure— exploring **tropical** rain forests around the world. We put this book together from some of the blog posts we wrote on the way.

BARKO'S BLOG-TASTIC RAIN FOREST FACTS

Tropical rain forests mostly grow in three huge patches in South America, Africa, and Southeast Asia. There are also smaller forests in Papua New Guinea and Australia.

5

Steamy Weather

Posted by: Ben Blog | August 20 at 11:03 a.m.

We started our trip in the amazing Amazon rain forest in South America. It's very hot and sticky, and it will be the same tomorrow and the day after that. This is because **tropical** rain forests grow along the **equator**, where it's warm and **humid** all year.

BARKO'S BLOG-TASTIC RAIN FOREST FACTS

It rains almost every day in the rain forest, and there are often thunderstorms. I'm already dripping wet. This orangutan in Borneo is using a leaf as an umbrella.

Spot the Rain Forest

Posted by: Ben Blog | September 9 at 2:29 p.m.

Our next stop was Rwanda in Central Africa, where we explored this **cloud forest**. It gets its name because it grows high up on the side of a mountain and is often covered in clouds. The Amazon rain forest is called a lowland forest because it grows on low-lying land.

BARKO'S BLOG-TASTIC RAIN FOREST FACTS

Parts of a lowland forest sometimes flood when a river rises above its banks. The trees may stay underwater for many months. They make fantastic homes for hungry fish.

Floor to Ceiling Trees

Posted by: Ben Blog | September 26 at 7:07 a.m.

Staying in Central Africa, we are in the rain forest in Congo. Here on the forest floor, it's so dark and gloomy that it's tricky to get a good photo. The trees above grow in layers, depending on how tall they are. The tallest reach 200 feet (60 meters). That's eight times as tall as a house!

BARKO'S BLOG-TASTIC RAIN FOREST FACTS
The layer below the tallest trees is called the **canopy**. It's like a thick, green roof of leaves and branches. About two-thirds of rain forest animals live in the canopy.

Fabulous Flowers

Posted by: Ben Blog | October 19 at 9:42 a.m.

I took a photo of this enormous flower in Sumatra, Southeast Asia. It's called a rafflesia, and it measures 3 feet (1 meter) across. Thousands of plants grow in the rain forest because it's so warm and wet. You would not want to get too close to this one, though—it smells like rotten meat!

bromeliad

BARKO'S BLOG-TASTIC RAIN FOREST FACTS

Not all rain forest plants grow in soil. Orchids and **bromeliads** grow high up on the branches of trees. They dangle their **roots** in the air to soak up moisture.

This pitcher plant also comes from Sumatra. It looks fabulous, but it's a killer. Its leaves are shaped like a pitcher, or jug, and they are very slippery. When an insect lands on the edge, it loses its footing and falls inside. Then the plant makes juices that **digest** the insect's body.

BARKO'S BLOG-TASTIC RAIN FOREST FACTS

Many tall rain forest trees have short roots for sucking water from the soil. To stop them from falling over, they grow huge extra roots from their trunks. These are called **buttress** roots.

Amazing Animals

Posted by: Ben Blog | December 5 at 6:19 p.m.

We headed back to South America to watch some wildlife. I couldn't wait! At least half of all the world's types of animals live in the rain forests. This tiny frog is a poison dart frog. Its bright colors look pretty, but they warn hungry birds that it's deadly poisonous.

BARKO'S BLOG-TASTIC RAIN FOREST FACTS

Jaguars are rain forest hunters from South America. They eat deer, tapir, turtles, caimans, and fish. Their teeth and jaws are so strong that they can bite through a turtle's shell. Yikes!

Our next stop was Madagascar, a large island off the coast of Africa. Its rain forests are home to chameleons, and they are amazing animals. They have very long, sticky tongues that they shoot out to catch insects, and big eyes that can swivel almost all the way around. How useful is that?!

BARKO'S BLOG-TASTIC RAIN FOREST FACTS

These mountain gorillas live in the **cloud forests** of Central Africa. They spend most of the day looking for food. At night, they sleep in beds they built from branches and leaves.

When I took a photo of this beauty in Java, Indonesia, I thought it was an orchid flower. Then I looked closer. It's actually an insect, called an orchid mantis. It's the same color as the orchid, and the flaps on its body look like petals. But, when an insect visits, the mantis snaps it up.

BARKO'S BLOG-TASTIC RAIN FOREST FACTS

In the Philippines, huge eagles soar through the tops of the tallest trees. They are looking for flying lemurs or monkeys to eat. They have big, hooked beaks and sharp claws for grabbing their **prey**.

Awesome Amazon

Posted by: Ben Blog | April 24 at 6:07 a.m.

This week, it was back to the Amazon rain forest. It's the world's biggest rain forest—almost the size of Australia—so there is still plenty to see. The rain forest grows on the banks of the Amazon River, so we are traveling by canoe. Some local rain forest people are coming along as guides.

BARKO'S BLOG-TASTIC RAIN FOREST FACTS

Sloths hang upside down from the trees, holding on with their hook-like claws. They spend most of the day fast asleep and only come down to the ground about once a week.

Riches of the Rain Forest

Posted by: Ben Blog | May 28 at 3:33 p.m.

Did you know that lots of everyday things come from the rain forest? They include fruit, spices, chocolate, coffee, and even chewing gum. Many plants make important medicines. This rosy periwinkle from Madagascar is used to treat people with a type of **cancer**.

BARKO'S BLOG-TASTIC RAIN FOREST FACTS

Tasty brazil nuts grow on tall trees in the Amazon rain forest. They grow inside huge pods, as big as coconuts. Each nut has a very hard shell, so you need to watch out for your teeth!

Rain Forests at Risk

Posted by: Ben Blog | June 7 at 5:11 p.m.

All over the world, people are destroying the rain forests. The forests are disappearing so quickly that there may be none left in 50 years. Here in Thailand, the forest is being cut down for **timber** and to make space for growing crops. It's a terrible sight.

These orangutans in Borneo lost their home when the rain forest was cut down. They were taken to a rescue center. The center has a patch of forest that is **protected**, and this is where the orangutans will live.

Steamy Rain Forests Quiz

If you are planning your own rain forest expedition, you need to be prepared. Find out how much you know about steamy rain forests with our quick quiz.

1. What is the weather like in the rain forest?
a) cold and icy
b) hot, wet, and sticky
c) windy

2. Where does a **cloud forest** grow?
a) on a mountain
b) by a river
c) in the desert

3. How tall are the tallest rain forest trees?
a) 20 feet
b) 200 feet
c) 2,000 feet

4. Which flower smells like rotten meat?
a) orchid
b) pitcher plant
c) rafflesia

5. Where is the biggest rain forest?
a) Africa
b) South America
c) Southeast Asia

6. Which of these comes from the rain forest?
a) chewing gum
b) coffee
c) chocolate

7. What is this?

8. What is this?

Answers

1. b
2. a
3. b
4. c
5. b
6. a, b, c
7. brazil nuts in a pod
8. jaguar's coat

29

Glossary

bromeliad plant that grows on tree branches in the rain forest

buttress prop or support

cancer disease that makes people very sick and can kill them

canopy thick roof of treetops over the rain forest

cloud forest rain forest that grows high up on a mountainside and is often covered in clouds

digest break down food into a liquid

equator imaginary line that runs around the middle of Earth

humid damp or moist

inquisitive interested in learning about the world

Marco Polo explorer who lived from about 1254 to 1324. He traveled from Italy to China.

prey animals that are hunted and eaten by other animals

protected saved from harm or damage

root part of a plant that grows into the ground to soak up water

timber wood used for building

tropical found in warm parts of the world

Find Out More

Books

Allgor, Marie. *Endangered Rain Forest Animals.*
New York: Rosen, 2013.

Amstutz, Lisa J. *Rain Forest Animal Adaptations.*
Mankato, Minn.: Capstone, 2012.

Bingham, Jane. *The Amazon* (Explorer Tales).
Chicago: Raintree, 2013.

Underwood, Deborah. *Hiding in Rain Forests.*
Chicago: Heinemann, 2011.

Web Sites

FactHound offers a safe, fun way to find Internet sites related to this book. All of the sites on FactHound have been researched by our staff.

Here's all you do:
Visit www.facthound.com
Type in this code: 9781432987794

Index